WETLAND

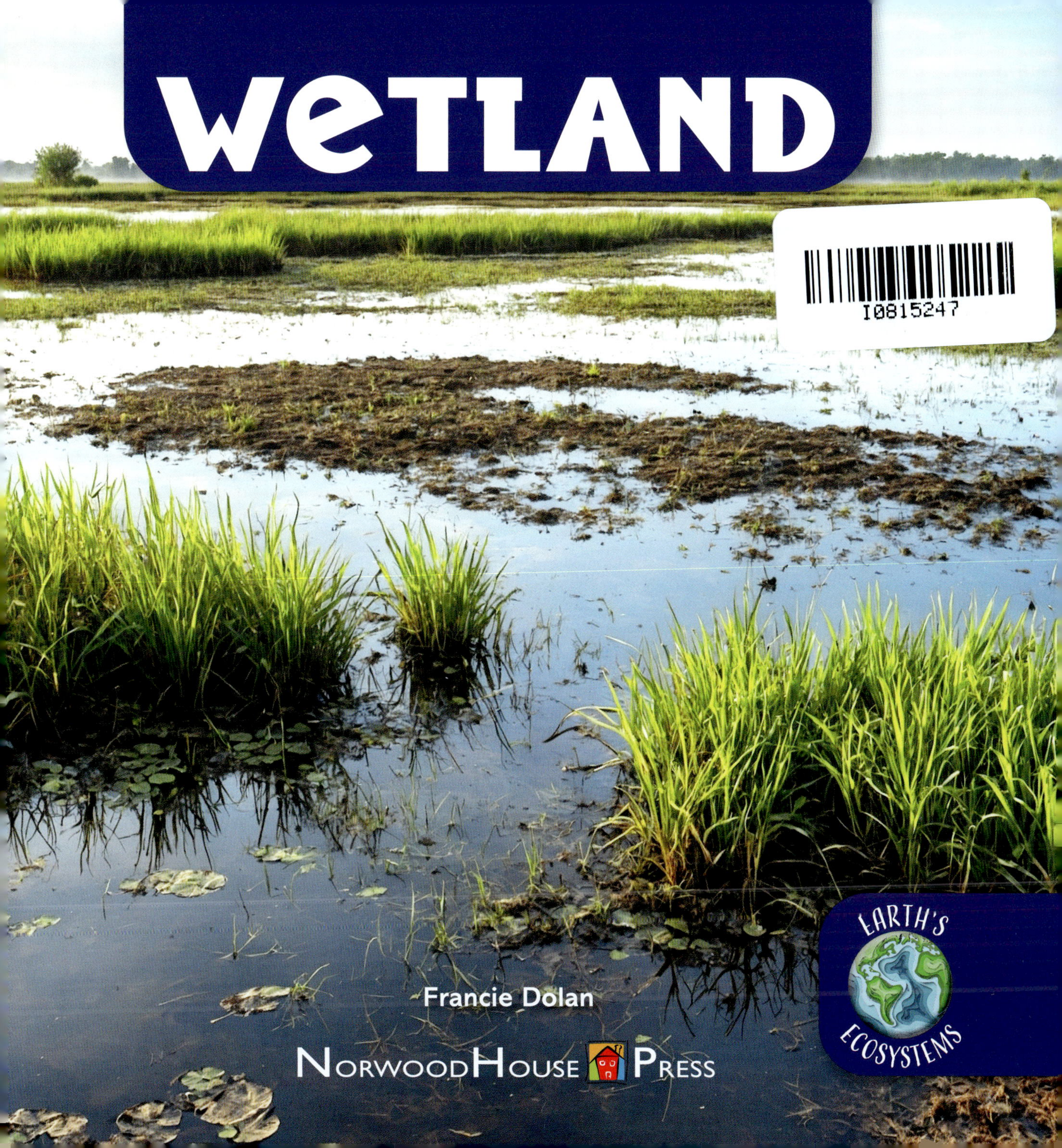

Francie Dolan

NorwoodHouse Press

Cataloging-in-Publication Data

Names: Dolan, Francie.
Title: Wetland / Francie Dolan.
Description: Buffalo, NY : Norwood House Press, 2026. | Series: Earth's ecosystems | Includes glossary and index.
Identifiers: ISBN 9781978577077 (pbk.) | ISBN 9781978577084 (library bound) | ISBN 9781978577091 (ebook)
Subjects: LCSH: Wetland ecology--Juvenile literature. | Wetland biodiversity--Juvenile literature.
Classification: LCC QH541.5.M3 D65 2026 | DDC 577.68--dc23

Published in 2026 by
Norwood House Press
2544 Clinton Street
Buffalo, NY 14224

Designer: Rhea Magaro
Editor: Kim Thompson

Photo credits: Cover, p. 1 Qasimphotographer, Kumer Oksa-na/Shutterstock.com; p. 3 Alex Manders/Shutterstock.com; p. 5 ZCOOL HelloRF/Shutterstock.com; pp. 6, 7 Bilanol/Shutterstock.com; p. 9 KelseyU/Shutterstock.com; p. 10 Audrey Snider-Bell/Shutterstock.com; p. 11 Damsea/Shutterstock.com; p. 12 Mariusz Bugno/Shutterstock.com; p. 13 Greg Amptman/Shutterstock.com; p. 15 Gordon Magee/Shutterstock.com; p. 16 Malgorzata Ksiazkie-wicz/Shutterstock.com; p. 18 Lutsenko_Oleksandr, Henk Vrieselaar/Shutterstock.com; p. 19 Brian Lasenby/Shutterstock.com; p. 20 Catcher of Light, Inc., jack perks/Shutterstock.com

Printed in the United States of America

CPSIA compliance information: Batch #CWNHP26: For further information contact Norwood House Press at 1-800-237-9932.

TABLE OF CONTENTS

The Wetland Ecosystem

Eco- means "home" or "environment." *System* means "a group of things that work together." Earth has many **ecosystems** that support life. Each is home to a network of living things that depend on each other.

One kind of ecosystem is a wetland. Wetlands are areas of land that are wet for at least part of the year. They are covered with water or have soil that is **saturated** with water. Swamps, marshes, and bogs are all wetlands.

Wetlands may be soaked with fresh water or salt water. The water may come from a spring or **aquifer**. It may be seawater that comes in at high tide.

Wetland ecosystems are important to Earth. They act like giant sponges to help control floods. They protect fragile coastlines and beaches.

Wetland Plants

Wetlands support a wide variety of plants. Special **adaptations** help them grow in soggy soil.

At high tide, saltwater marshes flood with salty ocean water. This is not a problem for saltmeadow cordgrass. Its leaves have glands that **secrete** salt and keep the plant healthy.

Submerged plant roots have trouble getting **oxygen**. The bald cypress tree has a solution. It has "knees" that stick above the water where there is air.

A mangrove tree's tall roots look like stilts. Soil collects and builds up around them. This helps the tree stay upright in the water.

Wetland Animals

Many animals depend on wetlands for food and shelter. They have adapted to life in a watery world.

Manatees use broad tails to steer through the water. A thick layer of **blubber** keeps them warm.

It is tough to fly with wet feathers. An egret wades on tall legs so its feathers stay dry. Its long bill probes the mud for insects. Long, skinny toes help the bird balance on muddy shores.

Frogs have webbed feet to help them swim. They can get the oxygen they need even when they are underwater. They breathe through their skin!

Wetland Food Chains

In a wetland, living things eat other living things in food chains. A mayfly might munch on a cattail. A frog may snap up the mayfly.

The frog might make a meal for a great blue heron. After the heron dies, **bacteria** will help it **decompose**.

All living things in wetland ecosystems depend on each other for survival. These places are important for plants, animals, and planet Earth.

Glossary

adaptations (ad-ap-TAY-shuhns): physical or behavioral changes that help plants and animals survive in their environment

aquifer (AH-kwuh-fer): an underground layer of rock or soil that holds water

bacteria (bak-TEER-ee-uh): microscopic, single-celled living things

blubber (BLUHB-ur): a layer of fat under the skin of a marine mammal

decompose (dee-kuhm-POZE): to rot or decay and return nutrients to the soil

ecosystems (EE-koh-sis-tuhms): natural communities where plants, animals, and their environment all work together

oxygen (AHK-si-juhn): a gas with no color that plant roots usually take in through pockets of air in the soil

saturated (SACH-uh-ray-tuhd): soaked through

secrete (si-KREET): to give off or release

submerged (suhb-MURJD): completely covered by water or another liquid

Thinking Questions

1. What is an ecosystem?
2. Why are wetlands important to Earth?
3. Give an example of an adaptation that helps wetland plants survive.
4. Give an example of an adaptation that helps wetland animals survive.
5. What does a food chain show?

Index

About the Author

Francie Dolan is continually amazed by the natural world and how Earth's plants, animals, and natural resources are interconnected. From her home near Seattle, Washington, she loves to hike and explore forests, lakes, mountains, and the seashore. When she gets home, she likes to draw and write about what she sees on her adventures.